PETER NAVARRO SENTENCED FOR STALLING CONGRESS

Who's Peter Navarro?

BY

Henry B. Hurd

TABLE OF CONTENT

Navarro Is Condemned to 4 Months in Jail for Stalling Congress
Our legislative issues columnists.

Conclusion

Introduction

Peter Kent Navarro is an American financial expert now utilized as the Colleague to the President and Head of Exchange and Assembling Strategy.

He has recently filled in as a Representative Right hand to the President and Overseer of the White House Public Exchange Board.

Initially from Massachusetts, Navarro got a Four-year certification in liberal arts degree from Tufts College before getting an Expert in Policy management and a PhD in financial matters from Harvard College.

He burned through three years in Thailand working for the US Harmony Corps. During the 1970s, he filled in as a political expert for a few state and government organizations.

Navarro started his scholarly vocation in 1981 at Harvard. Somewhere in the range of 1985 and 1988, he was a teacher at the College of California, San Diego, and the College of San Diego.

In 1989, he started his residency at the College of California, Irvine, where he is right now a teacher emeritus. He has been dynamic in governmental issues since the mid-1990s and has been important for the Donald Trump organization starting from the start.

Consistently, Navarro has delivered more than twelve books and companion looked into financial matters research on different subjects

Chapter 1:
Youth and Early Life

Brought into the world on July 15, 1949, in Cambridge, Massachusetts, USA, Navarro is the child of Alfred "Al" Navarro and Evelyn Littlejohn. His dad was a saxophonist and clarinetist and filled in as the frontman of a house band.

His mom filled in as a secretary at a Saks Fifth Road store. Following his parents' separation, he, alongside his sibling, was raised by his mom in Palm Ocean side, Florida, and Bethesda, Maryland.

After getting a secondary school confirmation, Navarro was selected at Tufts College on a full scholastic grant and got a B.A. degree in 1972. He then, at that point, served in the US Harmony Corps in Thailand.

After getting back to the US, he began going to Harvard College's John F. Kennedy School of Government. He accepted his Lord of Policy Implementation degree in 1979. In 1986, Navarro got his Ph.D. in financial aspects from Harvard under the oversight of Richard E. Caves.

Early Profession

During the 1970s, Peter Navarro was a strategy examiner for the Metropolitan Administrations Gathering, the Massachusetts Energy Office, and the US Branch of Energy.

Starting from the start of his vocation, he has kept up with the idea that the US ought to be "hard on exchange, take action against licensed innovation robbery, charge Chinese products, battle Chinese mercantilism, [and] bring position home."

Profession in the Scholarly Community

In 1981, Peter Navarro joined Harvard's Energy and Natural Strategy Place as an exploration partner. He left that occupation in 1985 to educate at the College of California, San Diego, and the College of San Diego.

In 1989, he turned into a financial aspects and public approach teacher at the College of California, Irvine. After showing there for a very long time, he currently holds a teacher emeritus status

Profession in Governmental issues

Peter Navarro has fruitlessly challenged for office in San Diego, California, multiple times. In 1992, he challenged the mayoral decisions. He got 38.2% votes in the primary, completing first. Nonetheless, he was crushed in the overflow by Susan Golding.

He likewise ran for the San Diego city gathering in 1993, the San Diego Province Leading group of Bosses in 1994, the 49th Legislative Region as the Leftist alliance candidate in 1996, and the Area 6 San Diego city chamber seat in 2001.

While Navarro had recently campaigned for office on Fair tickets and advocated Vote-based causes, he turned into a financial arrangement counselor to Donald Trump's 2016 official mission.

He worked together with the worldwide confidential value financial backer Wilbur Ross on composing a monetary arrangement for Trump's mission in September 2016. In October 2016, the paper 'Monetary Examination of Donald Trump's Agreement with the American Elector', which he co-composed with Wilbur Ross and Andy Puzder, was distributed.

In December 2016, after Donald Trump was chosen to be the 45th US President, he picked Navarro to act as the overseer of the White House Public Exchange Committee, a place that was recently set up. In April 2017, his office was assimilated into the Workplace of Exchange and

Assembling Strategy, of which Navarro was made the chief.

His perspectives on financial aspects and exchange are not a piece of the standard. A firm pundit of the exchange strategies of China and Germany, he has been a vocal supporter of decreasing US import/export imbalances.

He has made proposals for developing the American assembling area, setting high duties, and "localizing worldwide inventory chains". He is additionally extremely frank in his resistance toward the North American International Alliance and Transoceanic Organization.

Abstract Works

Peter Navarro has created more than twelve books, including 'The Approaching China Wars (2006) and 'Demise by China (2011). In 2012, he made a narrative on the last option book. The film has a similar title as the book, and entertainer Martin Sheen fills in as the storyteller on it.

He has additionally placed out peer-evaluated articles on subjects like exchange, energy strategy, noble cause, liberation, and the financial matters of garbage assortment.

Chapter 2
Peter Navarro's Better Half PETER

Navarro's better half Leslie Lebon petitioned for legal separation in 2018, with the one-time power couple fighting over an arrangement.

Here's the beginning and end you want to be familiar with Leslie Lebon, the ex of President Donald Trump's previous exchange guide Peter Navarro.
Leslie Lebon is not generally hitched to Peter Navarro

Who is Peter Navarro's ex?

Brought into the world on Walk 6, 1961, Leslie LeBon is a modeler by calling.

She previously came into the spotlight during Trump's administration, as the spouse of Navarro.

Leslie has a child named Alexander Navarro. Nonetheless, she had him with her past spouse, Greg LeBon.

Alex and his dad are both sandcastle stone carvers.

It isn't clear if she has a kid with Navarro.

Leslie is the organizer behind LeBon Draftsmen and remodeled the home she partook in the lower Nyes, upper Victoria Ocean side region with her better half Peter before their marriage separated.

Leslie worked for LeBon Draftsmen from 2001 until 2021 and has worked for LeBon Properties - an organization that fails to meet expectations for multi-family private properties - beginning around 2013.

Is Peter Leslie actually wedded?

Following 20 years of marriage, Peter and Leslie formally separated on December 31, 2020.

The couple - who wedded in 2001 - had subtly been engaged with an extended and unpleasant separation process starting around 2018.

As per the Everyday Mail, LeBon requested a separation in 2018 because of beyond-reconciliation issues
Following the separation interaction's fulfillment, Leslie has been given a portion of Peter's annuity benefits.

She has likewise parted the sum they partook in various ledgers similarly with her ex.

To evenhandedly appropriate their abundance, the two players deferred their privileges to spousal help.

Peter Navarro youngsters meet child Alex Navarro
He filled in as an Aide to the President, Overseer of Exchange and Assembling Strategy, and

strategy facilitator for the Public Protection
Creation Act in the Trump organization.

He was beforehand a Delegate Partner to the
President and Overseer of the White House
Public Exchange Chamber, a recently made
White House Office until it was integrated into
the Workplace of Exchange and Assembling
Strategy, a new position laid out by chief request
in April 2017.

Did Peter Navarro have a girl?

The couple have no girl together.
Who is the mother of Peter Navarro's child?
Leslie Lebon is a planner. She is notable for
being Peter Navarro's better half and Alex
Navarro's mom. More data about her is obscure.

Peter Navarro's ethnic foundation

Peter Navarro is a White American initially
hailing from Cambridge, Massachusetts. His

instructive excursion took him to Tufts College, where he procured a degree in financial matters.

Therefore, he sought cutting-edge examinations at Harvard College, getting an expert's in policy management and a Ph.D. in financial aspects.

Navarro, whose vocation reached out to past governmental issues, filled in as a business teacher at the College of California — Irvine for more than 25 years.

His striking introduction to the public eye was initiated with his 1998 book, "Demise by China," a scrutinization of China's exchange strategies. This distribution was ultimately adjusted into an honor-winning narrative film displayed at different film celebrations.

Throughout the long term, Navarro kept on distributing books zeroed in on exchange, including "The Approaching China Battles" in 2006, a work that got acclaim from previous

President Trump, who thought of it as one of his top choices.

Trump's appreciation for Navarro's perspectives on exchange at last prompted his meeting with the White House. At first, Navarro filled in as the Partner to the President and later expected the job of Head of Exchange and Assembling Strategy for the Trump organization.

In his own life, Navarro was hitched to modeler Leslie LeBon for almost twenty years, however, the couple separated in 2020.

Following his conviction on Thursday, Peter Navarro, remaining external to the Washington DC court, communicated his aim to pursue the decision.

He fought that his refusal to regard the summon was legitimate, referring to a 50-year-old Division of Equity strategy that senior White House authorities were not expected to affirm before Congress.

Previous President Donald Trump likewise said something regarding the conviction through a post on Truth Social, scrutinizing House Board head Nancy Pelosi and stating that Peter Navarro's declaration could never have fundamentally affected the examination.

Chapter 3
Peter Navarro Ethnicity

Peter Navarro is an American by ethnicity, hailing from the US. He was brought up in Cambridge, Massachusetts, and has spent a lot of his life serving his country in different jobs, including as a monetary consultant to previous President Donald Trump.

As an American resident, Navarro has profoundly participated in American governmental issues, financial matters, and public strategy all through his vocation.

Peter Navarro Nationality

Peter Navarro's nationality is White. He is of Caucasian descent, and his family foundation isn't known to be related to a particular ethnic gathering or legacy beyond being by and large sorted as White or Caucasian in the US.

Navarro's vocation has been essentially centered around financial matters, exchange strategy, and governmental issues, instead of his ethnic foundation, which is certainly not a conspicuous part of his public personality.

Peter Navarro Instruction

Peter Navarro's instructive excursion is set apart by an amazing scholarly foundation. He set out on his way to information with a degree in financial matters from Tufts College.

Following this undergrad achievement, he proceeded with his quest for scholarly greatness at one of the country's most renowned organizations, Harvard College.

At Harvard, Peter Navarro participated in cutting-edge examinations, prompting the fulfillment of a graduate degree in policy implementation. His scholarly excursion didn't end there, as he facilitated his instructive interests to accomplish a Ph.D. in financial matters from a similar prestigious foundation.

These instructive qualifications highlight Navarro's obligation to figure out monetary elements and public strategy.

Navarro's instructive establishment, advanced by his encounters at Tufts and Harvard, laid the basis for his ensuing professional trials, remembering his effective job as a financial counsel for the Trump organization.

His scholarly accomplishments have without a doubt added to his capacity to shape financial and exchange strategies while offering informed experiences on these basic matters.

Peter Navarro Total assets

Peter Navarro Total assets: An Investigate the Fortune of a Powerful Financial expert
In the realm of financial matters and legislative issues, Peter Navarro is a name that frequently

surfaces because of his critical commitments and impact.

As a financial expert, creator, and previous guide to President Donald Trump, Navarro considerably affects forming public and global monetary strategies.

Past his expert achievements, many are charmed by his fortune and total assets. In this article, we dig into Peter Navarro's total assets, revealing insight into his monetary achievement and giving five captivating realities about his abundance.

Assessed Total assets
Starting around 2023, Peter Navarro's total assets are assessed to be around $20 million. While this figure might fluctuate because of steadily changing economic situations and individual ventures, Navarro's total assets place him among the more elite classes of financial specialists.

Scholarly Accomplishments

Navarro's mastery of financial aspects can be credited to his hearty scholarly foundation. He holds a Ph.D. in financial matters from Harvard College, which without a doubt assumed a significant part in molding his profession and adding to his total assets.

 His broad information in the field has gained him acknowledgement and appreciation in the financial local area.

Origin and Distributions

Aside from his warning job, Navarro has written various books on financial matters, further establishing his standing as a vital figure in the field.

Outstanding distributions incorporate "The Approaching China Wars," "Passing by China," and "Hunching Tiger: How China's Militarism Affects the World."

These works mirror his aptitude as well as added to his general total assets through eminences and book deals.

Taxpayer supported organization

Navarro's contribution to taxpayer-supported organizations without a doubt had an impact on his monetary achievement.

Filling in as the Overseer of the White House Public Exchange Board under President Trump, he was a central member in forming exchange strategies and discussions. Such jobs frequently accompany rewarding compensations and advantages, adding to Navarro's total assets.

Speculation Adventures

Past his intellectual and political undertakings, Navarro has likewise wandered into speculation exercises. While explicit subtleties of his ventures are not openly uncovered, it is realized that he has taken vital actions in the financial exchange and land areas.

 These speculations, joined with his financial ability, have likely added to the development of his total assets.
Presently, we should resolve a few normal inquiries concerning Peter Navarro's total assets: How did Peter Navarro store up his abundance?

Navarro's abundance is principally a consequence of his effective profession as a financial expert, creation, taxpayer-supported organization, and speculation adventures.

What is Peter Navarro's essential type of revenue?
While his essential type of revenue might have differed all through his vocation, it probably originates from a blend of book eminences, government compensations, and speculation returns.

Did Peter Navarro acquire any abundance?

There is no open data accessible to propose that Navarro acquired any critical riches.

How have Navarro's total assets changed after some time?
Navarro's total assets have likely experienced variances over the long run because of economic situations, venture results, and changes in his expert jobs.

What effect did Navarro's job in the Trump organization have on his total assets?
Navarro's part in the Trump organization furnished him with rewarding compensation and a potential chance to shape strategies, which probably added to his total assets.

Are there any contentions encompassing Navarro's riches?
There have been no remarkable discussions concerning the gathering of Peter Navarro's riches.

Does Navarro give to worthy missions?
While explicit data regarding Navarro's magnanimous commitments isn't promptly accessible, numerous well-known people with significant abundance take part in humanitarian exercises.

Has Navarro confronted any monetary mishaps?
Freely accessible data demonstrates no critical monetary mishaps in Navarro's vocation.

How do Navarro's total assets contrast with different market analysts?
Navarro's total assets place him among the more affluent financial experts, even though there is extensive variety inside the field.

Does Navarro have any monetary interests in China?

Explicit subtleties of Navarro's ventures are not openly revealed, making it hazy whether he has any monetary interests in China.

What effect did Navarro's books have on his total assets?

Navarro's books have likely added to his total assets through book deals, eminences, and expanded acknowledgment inside the financial local area.

.

Does Navarro have any monetary interests in the financial exchange?

While it is realized that Navarro has taken key actions in the securities exchange, explicit subtleties of his ventures are not freely accessible.

Has Navarro given any monetary guidance or meetings?

Navarro has been known to offer financial exhortation and meetings, albeit the degree of his inclusion and any related expenses are not freely revealed.

How do Navarro's total assets contrast with other political consultants?

Navarro's total assets are moderately high contrasted with numerous political counselors, mirroring his persuasive job and fruitful vocation in financial matters.

All in all, Peter Navarro's total assets of roughly $20 million in 2023 are a demonstration of his prosperity as a financial specialist, creator, and previous counselor to President Trump.

 His scholarly accomplishments, distributions, taxpayer-driven organization, and speculation adventures have all added to his riches, hardening his situation as a noticeable figure in financial matters

Chapter 4
Navarro Is Condemned to 4 Months in Jail for Stalling Congress

Peter Navarro, an exchange consultant to previous President Donald J. Trump who assisted lay plans with keeping Mr.

Trump, in office after the 2020 political race, was condemned on Thursday to four months in jail for resisting a summons from the House board exploring the Jan. 6, 2021, assault on the Legislative center.

Mr. Navarro, 74, was found liable in September for two misdeed counts of criminal contempt of Congress, making him the second Trump associate to have to deal with damages connected with one of the central examinations concerning the State House revolt.

The adjudicator supervising the case, Amit P. Mehta, had dismissed Mr. Navarro's essential guard: that Mr. Trump had by and by guided him

not to help out the summon, and that he accepted
he was protected by chief honor.

"The words 'leader honor' are not otherworldly
spells," Judge Mehta said in giving over the
sentence after a strained more than two-hour
hearing in which he over and again disagreed
with Mr. Navarro's case of chief honor.

"It's anything but an escape prison free card," he
said.
In an irritable trade with Mr. Navarro's legal
counselors ahead of time, the adjudicator singled
out Mr.

Navarro's choice to spurn the summon even as
different helpers to Mr. Trump arranged whether
to consent. "I have a lot of regard for your client
and what he's accomplished expertly, I do," he
said.

"Which makes it all the more seriously
disheartening how he acted."

Seemingly shocked by Judge Mehta's reactions to one of his legal counselors Mr. Navarro at one point rose to represent himself, against what he said was his legal counselors' recommendation.

Relating his perspective when he got the summon, Mr. Navarro said that he was torn about whether to participate and that he had trusted his case would turn into a diagram for White House assistants summoned by Congress.

"All they need to do is peruse the record of you here today and they'll know what to do, sir," he said. "I didn't have any idea what to do."

Mr. Navarro was likewise requested to pay a $9,500 fine. He will avoid prison for the time being, essentially until Judge Mehta concludes whether he can stay free while he requests his conviction.

Outside Government Region Court in Washington, Mr. Navarro, encompassed by correspondents and cameras on an unexpectedly warm day, was quickly overwhelmed by harassers blowing whistles and jarring with his legal counselors for space behind him to display signs.

Over the commotion, Mr. Navarro insubordinately requested gifts for his lawful guard, adding that he was "not expecting or expecting" an exoneration from Mr. Trump.

Would it be a good idea for him to be reappointed to the administration?
Mr. Navarro, a Harvard-prepared financial specialist and a vocal pundit of China, filled in as an exchange guide to Mr. Trump before turning his concentration to the pandemic reaction.

After the 2020 political decision, notwithstanding, he progressively investigated ways of undermining the result of the race and keeping Mr. Trump in power.

Alongside Stephen K. Bannon, a long-term consultant to Mr. Trump, Mr. Navarro concocted an arrangement known as the Green Inlet Clear. Under the system, they would attempt to defer the certificate of the political decision by convincing conservative legislators to over and over challenge the outcomes in different swing states and apply strain on previous VP Mike Pence to ruin the result.

 He likewise cast uncertainty on the consequences of the race, gathering examples of implied inconsistencies and giving a three-section report guaranteeing political decision extortion as a component of what he depicted as a "perfect double-dealing."

For a long time, Mr. Navarro straightforwardly commended his planning, sharing subtleties of the arrangement in his 2021 diary and a meeting with Drifter magazine.

Our legislative issues columnists.

Times writers are not permitted to support or lobby for up-and-comers or political causes. That incorporates taking part in conventions and giving cash to a competitor or cause.

Those endeavors at last inspired the consideration of the House board, which looked for records and declarations from Mr. Navarro.

At the point when the board contacted Mr. Navarro, he quickly answered by email, expressing as if it were "chief honor" and never helping out the board.

In the wake of casting a ballot to hold Mr. Navarro in disdain, the House alluded to making a difference to the Equity Division, which got a fantastic jury prosecution.

Judge Mehta noticed the distinction between Mr. Navarro's public appearances and his reaction to Congress.

"You're glad to converse with the press about what you composed in your book, however not go up to the Slope and converse with Congress, which examination occurred and the reasons for that day," he said.

Mr. Navarro's legal counsel had requested a half-year probation and an insignificant fine. His excusal of the House board of trustees was a misconception, they fought, adding that Mr. Navarro had trusted that Mr. Trump had summoned chief honor.

In requesting a more permissive sentence, his legal counselors said the case had depended on cloudy and disrupted lawful inquiries regarding leader honor and the complicated division of abilities among Congress and the White House — questions that Judge Mehta had attempted to unwind over long stretches of suit before the preliminary.

We're nevertheless a refueling break in our excursion to understanding what leader honor means and how it ought to be summoned," Stanley Woodward Jr., a legal counselor for Mr. Navarro, said on Thursday.

"This case is nowhere near finished," he added. Judge Mehta seethed at the idea, noticing that others in Mr. Trump's circle had followed the House advisory group's summons.

"Any attorney deserving at least moderate respect," he answered irately, would have prompted Mr. Navarro "to draw in with Congress and sort out what is covered and what isn't covered."

Judge Mehta additionally addressed Mr. Woodward's affirmation that Mr. Navarro had acknowledged liability regarding his activities and was simply attempting to explain the law encompassing leader honor.

Judge Mehta referred to gathering pledges messages and news meetings outside the court in which Mr. Navarro condemned the Jan. 6 board

as "homegrown psychological oppressors" and a
"fake court."

"That kind of assertion from somebody ought to
realize better that adds to why our governmental
issues are so destructive," Judge Mehta said.

Mr. Bannon, who went out in 2017, was
sentenced on almost indistinguishable scorn
charges in 2022 and condemned to four months
in jail. He, as well, stays free as his allure pushes
ahead.

Conclusion
Peter Navarro's Height

As far as actual height, Peter Navarro remains at a typical level of 5 feet 9 inches (1.75 meters). Also, at the hour of composing, he gauged something like 62 kilograms (136 pounds).

Peter is confused with a non-white American given his family name. As recently referenced, race is a hostile subject on which Peter likewise showed up. In a meeting with CNN, Peter said that he was a small kid, perhaps around 8 years of age when he previously became mindful of racial issues.

An excursion to Woolworth's, where he saw a drinking fountain marked "Shaded," which he thought gave "hued water."

Virtual entertainment

With regards to web-based entertainment, Peter Navarro simply is by all accounts on Twitter.

Toward the finish of 2021, he had 70.7k adherents on the site. Besides that, Peter is uninterested in taking part in virtual entertainment. This makes sense as to why he isn't on Facebook or Instagram.

9 798877 509658